cooking in
Cast Iron

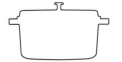

cooking in Cast Iron

Recipes **Valerie Aikman-Smith**

Photographs **Ray Kachatorian**

weldon**owen**

It's hard not to fall in love with the durability, even heat distribution, and distinctive beauty that have made cast iron a favorite among home cooks and restaurant chefs alike. My cast iron pots and pans remain my preferred cookware in the kitchen. Cast iron offers a return to a traditional way of cooking, free of gimmicks, focused on delicious results. Both traditional black cast iron and the colorful, enamel-coated variety prove amazingly versatile, whether simmering a hearty soup, preparing a savory main, or even creating a sweet dessert to end the meal. I find, too, that these beautiful vessels are perfect for casual entertaining, and I often bring them straight to the table for serving to my friends and family. I hope you will enjoy the recipes that follow, which aim to showcase the best capabilities of this time-honored cookware, with an eye towards simple, delicious, and foolproof dishes that are relevant to today's home cook.

Valerie Aikman-Smith

about cast-iron cookware

Cooks have long appreciated cast-iron cookware, whether classic black frying pans and dutch ovens or enameled pots finished in vibrant colors. There are sound reasons why cast iron is a favorite. The material is remarkably durable, and it performs extraordinarily well. These qualities underscore how cast-iron cookware is one of the best investments you can make for your kitchen.

9

what is cast iron?

The process of producing cast-iron cookware today is largely similar to the method used throughout history. Molten iron is poured into individual molds, which are left to cool until the iron hardens and the pans can be released. They are then left as is, or enameled, creating the two main types of cookware that are available: traditional cast iron and enameled cast iron.

Traditional cast iron is recognizable by its natural black color. These pans must be "seasoned," that is, the porous metal treated with oil to maintain its appearance and to create a stick-resistant surface. Enameled cast iron has been coated with a ceramic glaze that gives the surface its stick resistance. Colorful exterior glazes make these vessels as attractive as they are sturdy.

Both professional and home cooks have come to favor cast iron because of its desirable heating capabilities. Few metals rival cast iron's near-perfect heat distribution, and no other material can be heated on the stove top or in the oven to as high a temperature. This property makes cast

iron the material of choice for searing and sautéing. Steady heat distribution also makes a cast iron pan well-suited for deep-frying: it can maintain oil at a consistent temperature for long periods of time, resulting in evenly browned foods. Likewise, cast iron is an excellent material for braising. Tightly sealed pots maintain gentle heat over many hours for cooking succulent, flavorful stews and braises. Additionally, desserts such as cobblers and crumbles, as well as yeast breads, can be baked in cast-iron pans.

Cast-iron cookware is further valued for its remarkable durability. Used and maintained correctly, it can last beyond a lifetime. Cooks fortunate to inherit a pan from a relative know that traditional cast iron can even improve over generations. Although some enameled cast-iron pans cost more than nonstick pans, they tend to last far longer and are less prone to scratching, making them well worth the investment.

From dutch ovens and braisers to frying and grill pans to baking pans and roasters, cast-iron may be the only cookware collection you need.

types of cast-iron cookware

Versatile cast-iron cookware serves many purposes. You can cook any recipe in your repertoire with a cast-iron dutch oven, frying pan, grill pan, or baking pan. Understanding the two basic types of cookware and being aware of the many shapes and sizes are useful when either selecting a new piece in the store or figuring out what pan to enlist for preparing dinner tonight.

traditional & enameled cast iron Classic black frying pans, dutch ovens, and other traditional cast iron pots and pans have long graced home kitchens. Heavy and durable, the material may be slightly rough to the touch. Traditional cast iron heats up slowly, but retains and distributes heat extremely well. It can reach a higher temperature than any other cookware material and is never toxic, unlike nonstick coatings, which release toxins when heated beyond a certain temperature. Even if you happen to scrape off a tiny flake from a cast-iron pan, it is harmless to ingest. Cast iron must be seasoned before use. Today, however, nearly all traditional cast-iron pans are sold preseasoned and require minimal care to maintain (see page 16).

Cast-iron cookware with a hard enamel coating glazed on the surface has the same heating advantages as traditional cast iron. The enameled surface makes these pieces generally easier to clean and more stick resistant than their traditional counterparts. High-acid ingredients can react with traditional cast iron and impart a slightly metallic flavor to foods. If you are cooking with wine, vinegar, tomatoes, or citrus, enameled cast iron is a better choice. Many cooks appreciate enameled cast iron because the colorful pieces can be brought from the kitchen to the table for serving.

dutch ovens & braisers Available in a round or oval shape, dutch ovens have tight-fitting lids and, often, looped handles on opposite sides. These pots are made for slow cooking, and the ingredients can be sautéed or browned before they are simmered or braised in the same pot. A dutch oven is also an excellent choice for deep-frying, as the high sides help prevent hot oil from splattering beyond the pot. With the exception of miniature, single-serving pots, they range in capacity from 2 quarts (2 l) to 13 quarts (13 l). The 6- or 7-quart (6- or 7-l) size is the most versatile for the average household.

Variations on the dutch oven include braisers and tagines. Braisers are generally wider and shallower than dutch ovens. They have rounded sides and domed lids to encourage condensed liquids to run back into the food as it cooks.

A tagine is a braiser specifically designed to cook a North African stew of the same name. It consists of a shallow circular pan with a conical lid to trap moisture and allow it to drip back onto the slowly cooking food.

frying pans If told that they could keep only one pan in their collection, many cooks would choose a classic cast-iron frying pan. These long-handled pans with sloping sides range from 6 inches (15 cm) to 16 inches (40 cm) in diameter. Many feature a second small handle and a notch in one or both sides for pouring liquids. In addition to their proficiencies in sautéing and searing, cast-iron frying pans, both traditional and enameled, are perfect for oven cooking. Their effective heat distribution helps cook foods evenly, and the handles are safe for use in the oven.

grill pans Resembling square, rectangular, or round frying pans, grill pans have a notable addition—ridges on the cooking surface that create pleasing grill marks on meats, poultry, vegetables, and sandwiches. The elevated ridges also help drain fat from food as it cooks. Some manufacturers offer an accessory for the grill pan, a *mattone*, or "brick," used to weight foods, such as a butterflied chicken or Italian-style grilled sandwiches, so that they cook quickly and evenly.

baking, roasting & gratin pans Other types of cast-iron pans are designed for oven use. Rectangular pans of various dimensions are indispensable for cooking lasagne and other baked dishes, including desserts, and for roasting a wide range of meats, poultry, and vegetables. Gratin pans are shallow, either round or oval in form, and have slightly slanted sides. This shape exposes the maximum surface area to the oven's dry heat in order to develop a crunchy, browned topping on baked foods.

worth its weight

People new to using cast iron sometimes complain about the material's weight. Wise home cooks and professionals, however, recognize weight as the true mark of value. Cast iron shouldn't be as light as a nonstick or aluminum pan—you should be suspicious if it is. On the other hand, quality cast iron is never heavy to the point that a pan is difficult to lift or unwieldy to handle. The best manufacturers develop their cookware so that it is just the right weight: substantial enough to reach and retain high temperatures, but light enough not to be an inconvenience in the kitchen.

how to use cast iron

As the recipes in this book demonstrate, cast iron is an excellent material for any cooking technique, whether simmering or braising, sautéing or deep-frying, pan-grilling or roasting. The advice below for heating and cooling pans and bringing them to the table will help ensure that you'll get the best performance from your cookware and the best results for your recipe.

cook tops Cast iron works equally well on gas or electric stove tops. Some manufacturers of glass cook tops caution against using cast iron, as it can scratch the clear surface, but others claim it can be used with careful handling. Cast-iron cookware also works well on induction cook tops, an increasingly popular and energy efficient type of cook top, which uses electro-magnetic energy to generate heat.

preparing to cook Before cooking, be sure to remove any labels from new cookware pieces, and then wash and dry pans or pots thoroughly. If you plan to put the cookware in the oven, check the manufacturer's instructions for guidance on maximum oven temperatures or other restrictions.

preheating Like with most cookware, it is wise to preheat cast-iron pots or pans before cooking to ensure good results. Heavy cast iron requires a longer time to become hot enough for cooking than other cookware materials. When you start a recipe on the stove top, plan on 1 to 3 minutes to preheat a pan before adding the first ingredients.

testing a pan's heat To test if a cast-iron pan has sufficiently preheated for cooking, sprinkle a few drops of water on the surface. If they pop and sputter, the pan has begun to warm. To distinguish between different heat levels, place hand just over a dutch oven or frying pan's cooking surface. For low heat, you should be able to hold your hand comfortably over the pan for 5 seconds; for medium heat, 3 to 4 seconds. When deep frying in cast iron, always use a deep-frying thermometer to ensure the oil is at the optimum heat for frying. For a grill pan, a few slight wisps of smoke are a good a sign that the pan is at the right temperature to create the desired pronounced browned grill marks on the cooking food.

Thanks to cast iron's superior heat-retention properties, cookware manufacturers generally recommend using a lower heat for cooking than you might on another cookware material. If you feel you need a higher heat than is called for in a recipe, increase the heat gradually, knowing that it can take up to a minute or more for the temperature to increase to the desired level.

cooking Nearly all cast-iron pots and pans are designed for use both on the stove top and in the oven. This means that you can start by searing or sautéing on the stove top and then put the same pan into the oven to bake, roast, simmer, or braise the food. The knobs on the lids of certain dutch ovens may be recommended only for oven temperatures up to 375°F (190°C), but since most oven-braising takes place at 350°F (180°C) or lower, this rarely limits use. If the knobs or handles on cookware are made from a different material than the pan, check the manufacturer's specifications before using in a hot oven or under the broiler. When using cast-iron pans in the oven, remember that, like the rest of the pot, the handles or knobs will get very hot. Always be sure to protect your hands with oven mitts or potholders.

utensils Because enameled coatings can scratch if you are not careful, use wooden or heatproof silicone spoons, spatulas, or other tools when cooking with enameled cast iron. It is fine to use metal spoons or spatulas when cooking with traditional cast iron.

cooling Just as a cast-iron pan takes extra time to heat up, it will take a bit longer than pans of other materials to cool down. This can be an asset when serving a dish directly from the pan, as the residual warmth will help keep the food at a good serving temperature. Remember to use protective mitts when touching hot handles and to elevate cast-iron cookware on a trivet to protect the counter or tabletop, or to hasten cooling. Always let cooked food cool to room temperature before storing it in the refrigerator

or freezer. Do not store food for long periods of time in traditional, unenameled cast iron, which could leach into the food and affect the flavor.

stove to table serving One of the benefits of cooking in cast iron is that the cookware can be brought to the table and the food served directly from it for a casual, family-style meal. A handful of recipes in this book call for small baking dishes, which can be presented at the table for individual servings. When serving from a cast-iron vessel, be sure to insulate the table with a trivet or folded kitchen towel and warn diners not to touch the hot dishes.

15

---

outdoor cooking

Cast-iron cookware is a popular choice for cookouts and camping. Durable frying pans and dutch ovens can be put directly on the cooking grate of a gas or charcoal grill to cook or heat foods while you are grilling another dish. Some old-fashioned dutch ovens feature a single wire handle, three small feet, and a slightly concave lid. These ovens are designed specifically for camping-style outdoor cooking: the feet hold the oven over hot coals, and more hot coals are heaped on the lid, in order to heat the pot from both top and bottom and imitate the effect of an oven. This type of cooking recalls the origin of the dutch oven, which dates back to the 1700s, when it was used exclusively over open flames or was nestled in hot coals and ash. Today, campers still like to make chili, biscuits, and other dishes by this time-tested method.

cleaning, maintenance & care

Cast-iron cookware is as easy to care for as it is to use. To ensure the performance and durability of your cookware, follow the tips here for cleaning and maintaining both types of cast iron. If you take these simple measures, your pans will last as long as those you may have inherited from a beloved family cook.

cleaning cast iron Traditional cast iron should not be cleaned in the dishwasher or be exposed to particularly harsh soap. Scrub a pan with a stiff brush, using hot water with a minimal amount of mild soap. For stubborn particles, you can soak the pan briefly, or boil some water in it for a few minutes and scrub again. Dry the pan immediately after washing to prevent rusting.

Enameled cast iron may be cleaned in the dishwasher, although to best preserve bright colors, some manufacturers recommend hand washing. Use soft brushes and sponges to prevent scratching the enameled surface. Avoid plunging any piece of hot cast iron into cold water, as the temperature difference could cause it to warp or crack.

seasoning The term seasoning refers to the process of creating a stick-resistant surface on traditional cast-iron pans and protecting the material from rusting. This is done by rubbing oil into the naturally porous surface or by heating a pan to help it absorb the oil (see box at right). A well-seasoned pan will have a deep black color and glossy sheen. Most traditional cast-iron pans

sold today are preseasoned, but you may need to re-season pans occasionally to maintain the cooking surface and combat rust.

storing Keep cast-iron cookware in a clean, dry place. If a traditional cast-iron pan begins to show signs of rust, don't despair. Simply scour the pan to remove the rust and then re-season thoroughly.

---

how to season traditional cast iron

If you are working with a new piece of unseasoned cookware, or food is noticeably sticking to the pan you already own, you need to season the pan. Line the bottom of the oven with aluminum foil, and preheat the oven to 350°F (180°C). Coat the clean, dry pan inside and out with a flavorless vegetable-based oil. Place the oiled pan upside down on the oven rack and bake for 1 hour. Turn the oven off and let the pan cool completely in the oven. The pan may smoke during this time; you may want to turn on your kitchen fan. It is best to refer to the manufacturer's instructions for the recommended method of re-seasoning a particular piece of cookware.

dutch ovens & braisers

A dutch oven is a cast-iron kettle with a tight-fitting cover that is used for slow cooking. Thought to come from the Pennsylvania Dutch community in the 1700s, these pots were originally developed to cook over an open flame or bury in the smoldering coals of a campfire. A braiser is similar, featuring gently sloping sides and a domed lid. Both are designed to cook food slowly in a moist, closed environment, which is perfect for flavorful chilis and stews, succulent braised chicken and short ribs, dark greens, and tough vegetables. Lids with specially designed spikes or ridges encourage condensation, keeping food moist as it cooks.

beef chili with black beans

¼ cup (2 fl oz/60 ml) olive oil

2 cloves garlic, minced

1 yellow onion, chopped

2 serrano chiles, finely chopped

1½ lb (750 g) lean ground beef

2 tablespoons pure ancho chile powder

1 teaspoon Spanish smoked sweet paprika or regular sweet paprika

2 teaspoons ground cumin

1 tablespoon chopped chipotle chiles in adobo sauce

2 tablespoons tomato paste

1 can (15 oz/470 g) crushed tomatoes with juice

1 cup (8 fl oz/250 ml) dry red wine

2 cans (15 oz/470 g each) black beans, drained

2 oz (60 g) bittersweet chocolate, finely chopped

Sea salt and cracked pepper

Grated sharp Cheddar cheese, sour cream, cilantro leaves, and sliced green onions for topping

MAKES 6 SERVINGS

In a 5½- to 7-qt (5.5- to 7-l) dutch oven over medium heat, warm the olive oil. Add the garlic, onion, and serrano chiles and sauté until the garlic and onions are tender and golden, about 4 minutes.

Add the beef and cook, stirring frequently and breaking up any larger pieces with a wooden spoon, until browned, 8–10 minutes.

Stir in the chile powder, paprika, cumin, and chipotle chiles. Add the tomato paste, tomatoes, and wine. Bring to a boil, stirring constantly. Reduce the heat to low, cover, and simmer, stirring occasionally, until the meat is cooked through and the chili has thickened slightly, about 30 minutes.

Add the black beans and chocolate, stirring until the chocolate melts. Cover the pot and continue cooking over low heat until the flavors are blended and the beans are heated through, about 15 minutes. Season to taste with salt and pepper.

Place the toppings in individual bowls. Ladle the chili into serving bowls and serve right away, passing the toppings at the table.

This is the ideal dish for a casual get-together, as everyone can customize their servings by adding their own choice of toppings. Dark chocolate gives the chili depth and balances the spicy seasonings. Serve with warm corn tortillas or corn muffins.

white bean & vegetable soup

¼ cup (2 fl oz/60 ml)
olive oil

2 cloves garlic,
 finely chopped

2 shallots, finely chopped

2 carrots, sliced

1 leek, white part
only, sliced

2 stalks celery, sliced

½ teaspoon red
pepper flakes

1 tablespoon chopped
fresh rosemary

2 tablespoons fresh
thyme leaves

Sea salt and cracked
black pepper

3 cups (6 oz/185 g)
roughly chopped spinach

6 large tomatoes, chopped

2 tablespoons
tomato paste

1 can (15 oz/470 g)
cannellini beans, drained

4 cups (32 fl oz/1 l)
chicken broth

Extra-virgin olive oil
for drizzling

Grated Parmesan
cheese for serving

MAKES 6–8 SERVINGS

In a 5½- to 7-qt (5.5- to 7-l) dutch oven over medium heat, warm the olive oil. Add the garlic, shallots, carrots, leek, and celery and sauté until golden brown, about 5 minutes.

Add the red pepper flakes, rosemary, and thyme and season lightly with salt and pepper. Add the spinach and stir until wilted, about 2 minutes. Add the tomatoes, tomato paste, and beans. Pour in the broth and bring to a boil. Reduce the heat to low and simmer uncovered, stirring occasionally, until the vegetables are tender, about 25 minutes.

Ladle the soup into bowls. Garnish each with a generous swirl of extra-virgin olive oil and a dusting of Parmesan. Serve right away.

This twist on Italian minestrone, with its hearty tomato base, is especially welcome in cold weather. The garnish of olive oil and grated Parmesan brings out the soup's flavor. The large capacity of a dutch oven holds the bounty of vegetables as it simmers in the savory broth.

braised greens with pancetta

3 tablespoons olive oil

1 clove garlic,
finely chopped

1 red onion,
finely chopped

½ lb (250 g) pancetta,
chopped

1½ teaspoons Spanish
smoked sweet paprika
or regular sweet paprika

1½–1¾ lb (750–875 g)
Tuscan kale, or another
kale variety (about
3 bunches), roughly
chopped

2 cups (16 fl oz/500 ml)
chicken broth

Sea salt and cracked
pepper

½ cup (3 oz/90 g) raisins

1 tablespoon balsamic
vinegar

MAKES 4–6 SERVINGS

In a braiser or dutch oven with at least a 4 qt (4 l) capacity, warm the olive oil over medium heat. Add the garlic and onion and sauté until soft and golden, about 5 minutes.

Add the pancetta and paprika and cook, stirring, until the pancetta is browned and crisp, about 5 minutes.

Working in batches, add the kale and stir until wilted, 8–10 minutes. Pour in the broth, stir, and season lightly with salt and pepper. Cover, reduce the heat to low, and simmer until the kale is tender but still slightly firm, about 15 minutes. Add the raisins, cover, and continue to cook until they have absorbed some of the juices and plumped up, about 15 minutes.

Remove from the heat and stir in the balsamic vinegar. Serve right away.

Slowly braising kale in a covered cast-iron pot makes for a rich, comforting dish. Pancetta and smoked paprika add an earthy flavor, while raisins contribute a slight sweetness. Turn this into a main dish for four by tossing it with 1 pound (500 g) of your favorite pasta.

olive oil–braised potatoes with herbs

3 tablespoons plus ¼ cup
(2 fl oz/60 ml) olive oil

1½ lb (750 g) baby
potatoes, cut in half

2 cloves garlic

1 sprig fresh rosemary

3 sprigs fresh thyme

Sea salt and cracked
pepper

Finely grated zest and
juice of 3 lemons

MAKES 4–6 SERVINGS

Preheat the oven to 375°F (190°C).

In a braiser or dutch oven with at least a 4 qt (4 l) capacity, warm the
3 tablespoons oil over medium heat. Add the potatoes, garlic, rosemary,
and thyme and sauté until golden, 8–10 minutes. Season with salt and
pepper. Add the ¼ cup olive oil and the lemon zest and juice. Stir well.

Cover the pot and bake the potatoes for 30 minutes. Remove from the oven,
uncover, and stir the potatoes. Return to the oven and bake, uncovered,
until the potatoes are tender and dark golden brown, about 10 minutes.
Serve right away.

A common technique in Mediterranean cuisine,
braising potatoes in an olive oil bath is a nice change
from roasting them. Cooking in a covered cast-iron
braiser preserves the delicate flavor of the rosemary
and thyme and accentuates the perfume of the lemon.

or

brussels sprouts with bacon & onions

5 tablespoons
(3 fl oz/80 ml) olive oil

3 cloves garlic,
finely chopped

1 tablespoon
mustard seeds

8 slices smoked
bacon, chopped

1½ lb (750 g) brussels
sprouts, trimmed

Sea salt and
cracked pepper

2 cups (16 fl oz/500 ml)
chicken broth

1 large yellow onion,
thinly sliced

2 tablespoons honey

MAKES 4–6 SERVINGS

In a braiser or dutch oven with at least a 4 qt (4 l) capacity, warm
3 tablespoons of the olive oil over medium-high heat. Add the garlic,
mustard seeds, and bacon and sauté until the bacon is golden brown
and crisp, 2–3 minutes.

Add the brussels sprouts and cook, stirring occasionally, until they begin
to turn golden brown, about 5 minutes. Season with salt and pepper. Pour
in the broth and bring to a boil. Reduce the heat to low, cover, and simmer
until tender, about 10 minutes.

Meanwhile, in a 10-inch (25-cm) frying pan over medium-high heat, warm
the remaining 2 tablespoons olive oil. Add the onions and sauté until dark
golden brown, about 5 minutes. Stir in the honey. Reduce the heat to low
and continue to cook, stirring occasionally, until the onions are soft and
caramelized, 5–8 minutes.

Uncover the brussels sprouts and cook until the liquid is reduced
by one-fourth, about 5 minutes.

Top the brussels sprouts with the caramelized onions and serve right away.

These brussels sprouts are slowly braised in broth to
mellow their bitter edge, then topped with honey-glazed
onions. Mustard seeds give the dish a little heat. Serve
with grilled or roasted meats or fish.

lamb tagine with apricots & pine nuts

2 lb (1 kg) boneless
lamb shoulder, cut into
1½-inch (4-cm) cubes

2 tablespoons chopped
preserved lemon peel

1 tablespoon grated
fresh ginger

1 tablespoon ground cumin

1 tablespoon coriander
seeds

1 teaspoon chili powder

½ teaspoon *each* ground
cloves and saffron threads

2 cups (16 fl oz/500 ml)
chicken broth

3 tablespoons olive oil

2 cloves garlic,
finely chopped

1 yellow onion,
finely chopped

1 jalapeño chile, seeded
and finely chopped

Sea salt and cracked pepper

1½ cups (9 oz/280 g) dried
apricots, soaked in water
for 30 minutes

1½ cups (6 oz/185 g)
pitted green olives

½ cup (2½ oz/75 g)
pine nuts, toasted

½ cup (½ oz/15 g) fresh
mint leaves, torn

MAKES 6 SERVINGS

In a nonreactive bowl, toss together the lamb, preserved lemon, ginger, cumin, coriander, chili powder, and cloves. Cover the bowl and set aside for 30 minutes. Meanwhile, place the saffron threads in a bowl, pour in the broth, and set aside.

In an 11-inch (28-cm) tagine, or a dutch oven or braiser with at least a 3 qt (3 l) capacity, warm the olive oil over medium-high heat. Add the garlic, onion, and chile and sauté until soft, about 3 minutes. Season lightly with salt and pepper.

Add the lamb mixture and cook, stirring frequently, until the meat is browned on all sides, about 3 minutes. Add the saffron mixture and bring to a boil. Reduce the heat to low, cover, and simmer, stirring occasionally, until the meat is tender, about 1 hour.

Add the apricots and olives and continue to cook, covered, until heated through, about 15 minutes. Remove from the heat. Let stand for 5 minutes.

Transfer the lamb to a large bowl and sprinkle with the pine nuts and mint. Serve right away.

This slow-cooked lamb stew infused with spices offers a taste of Morocco. The preserved lemon, used extensively in North African cuisine, is available from specialty-food markets. If you don't have a tagine, you can also prepare this in a braiser or dutch oven.

herbed beef stew

2 lb (1 kg) beef chuck, cut into 2-inch (5-cm) pieces

2 tablespoons all-purpose flour

Sea salt and cracked pepper

4 tablespoons (2 fl oz/60 ml) olive oil

2 cloves garlic, minced

2 shallots, finely chopped

2 tablespoons fresh winter savory leaves

2 tablespoons fresh thyme leaves

2 tablespoons fresh marjoram leaves

2 tablespoons fresh oregano leaves

1 sprig fresh rosemary

1 small turnip, peeled and cut into 2-inch (5-cm) pieces

2 parsnips, peeled and cut into 2-inch (5-cm) pieces

2 bottles (11 fl oz/ 324 ml each) stout, preferably Guinness

2 bay leaves

1 cup (5 oz/155 g) drained pickled cocktail onions

MAKES 6 SERVINGS

In a bowl, combine the beef and flour and toss to coat. Season lightly with salt and pepper and set aside.

In a 5½- to 7-qt (5.5- to 7-l) dutch oven over medium-high heat, warm 2 tablespoons of the olive oil. Add the garlic and shallots and sauté until soft, about 2 minutes. Season lightly with salt and pepper. Add the savory, thyme, marjoram, oregano, and rosemary and stir well. Add the turnip and parsnips and continue to cook, stirring, until the vegetables are golden brown, 3–4 minutes. Transfer to a plate and set aside.

Add the remaining 2 tablespoons oil to the pot. Add the beef and cook, stirring frequently, until the meat is well browned on all sides, 5–7 minutes total. Return the vegetables to the pot and stir well. Pour in the stout and add the bay leaves. Bring the liquid to a boil, reduce the heat to low, cover, and simmer until the meat and vegetables are tender, about 2 hours.

Stir in the onions and continue to simmer until the sauce has thickened slightly, about 30 minutes. Discard the bay leaves. Serve right away.

This slow-cooked stew with fall vegetables is seasoned with a quartet of aromatic herbs, lending a fresh taste to a cold-weather supper. The stout contributes a slightly sweet, nutty flavor, while the pickled onions add a tangy counterpoint. Serve over boiled potatoes.

chicken potpies

¼ cup (2 oz/60 g) unsalted butter, plus butter as needed

3 tablespoons olive oil

4 skinless, boneless chicken breast halves, cut into 1-inch (2.5-cm) pieces

2 cloves garlic, finely chopped

1 tablespoon chopped fresh rosemary

1½ tablespoons fresh thyme leaves

1 yellow onion, roughly chopped

1 fennel bulb with fronds, trimmed and roughly chopped

Sea salt and cracked pepper

1 cup (8 fl oz/250 ml) dry white wine

⅓ cup (2 oz/60 g) all-purpose flour

2 cups (16 fl oz/500 ml) whole milk, at room temperature

Two 9-inch (23-cm) squares frozen puff pastry, thawed

1 large egg, beaten

MAKES 4 SERVINGS

Preheat the oven to 400°F (200°C). Generously butter four 6½-inch (16.5-cm) cast-iron frying pans or round gratin dishes about 6 inches (15 cm) in diameter and set aside.

In a dutch oven or braiser with at least a 3 qt (3 l) capacity, warm the olive oil over medium-high heat. Add the chicken, garlic, rosemary, and thyme and sauté until coated with the oil, 2–3 minutes. Add the onion and fennel and season lightly with salt and pepper. Cook, stirring frequently, until the chicken and vegetables are golden, about 5 minutes. Pour in the wine, cover, and simmer until the chicken is tender and cooked through, about 5 minutes. Remove from the heat and set aside.

In a saucepan over medium heat, melt the butter. Stir in the flour and cook, stirring, for about 2 minutes. Stirring continuously, slowly add the milk and cook until the sauce is thick, about 4 minutes. Pour the sauce over the chicken mixture and stir until the ingredients are well combined. Season with salt and pepper. Divide among the prepared pans and set aside.

Lay the pastry sheets on a lightly floured work surface. Cut each sheet in half to make 4 pieces of pastry. Roll each piece out to roughly fit the diameter of the pans. Place 1 piece of pastry over each dish and tuck the edges down around the sides of the pan. Brush with the beaten egg.

Place the pans on a large baking sheet and bake until the pastry has risen and is golden brown, about 30 minutes. Serve right away.

Baking potpies in individual cast-iron frying pans or gratin pans is an appealing way to serve a favorite comfort food. This version adds sweet fennel and fresh herbs to the classic recipe and keeps things simple by using purchased puff pastry.

southern-style fried chicken

1 chicken, about 4 lb
(2 kg), cut into 10 pieces

1½ cups (12 fl oz/375 ml)
buttermilk

1 large egg

2 tablespoons Cajun
seasoning blend

Sea salt and
cracked pepper

1 cup (5 oz/155 g)
all-purpose flour

½ cup (2½ oz/75 g)
cornmeal

½ teaspoon sweet
paprika

Canola oil for frying

Lemon wedges
for serving

MAKES 6 SERVINGS

Arrange the chicken pieces in a nonreactive baking dish. In a bowl, whisk together the buttermilk, egg, 1 tablespoon of the Cajun seasoning, and ½ teaspoon each salt and pepper. Pour over the chicken pieces and turn to coat. Cover and refrigerate for at least 4 hours or up to overnight.

In large bowl, mix together the flour, cornmeal, the remaining 1 tablespoon Cajun seasoning, and the paprika. Season with salt and pepper. Set aside.

Preheat the oven to 350°F (180°C). Remove the chicken in its marinade from the refrigerator and bring to room temperature.

Pour the oil to a depth of at least 3 inches (7.5 cm) into a dutch oven with at least a 5 qt (5 l) capacity. Heat over medium heat until the oil registers 350°F (180°C) on a deep-frying thermometer. Place a wire rack over a rimmed baking sheet and set near the stove.

Working in batches, remove 3 or 4 chicken pieces from the marinade, letting the excess drip back into the bowl. Place each piece in the cornmeal mixture and turn to coat. Carefully slide the coated chicken into the hot oil and fry, turning with tongs, until dark golden brown, 5–7 minutes. Transfer the chicken to the wire rack. Return the oil to 350°F before frying the next batch. When all the chicken is cooked, put the baking sheet in the oven and bake the chicken until opaque throughout, about 10 minutes.

Remove the chicken from the oven and sprinkle with salt and pepper. Serve right away with the lemon wedges.

Cajun seasoning—a mixture of potent spices such as chiles, onion, garlic, and black pepper—gives this chicken a spicy kick. A dutch oven is practical for deep-frying, as it heats evenly, maintains the oil at an even temperature, and has high sides to prevent splattering.

classic pot roast

1 boneless chuck roast, about 4 lb (2 kg), tied

Sea salt and cracked pepper

2 tablespoons all-purpose flour

8 tablespoons (4 fl oz/ 125 ml) olive oil

1 garlic bulb, cut in half crosswise

1 yellow onion, roughly chopped

1 stalk celery, roughly chopped

1 carrot, roughly chopped

4 sprigs fresh thyme

3 sprigs fresh oregano

1 bay leaf

1 sprig fresh rosemary

5 cups (40 fl oz/1.25 l) beef broth

3 cups (24 fl oz/750 ml) dry red wine such as Cabernet Sauvignon

8 oz (250 g) chanterelle mushrooms, roughly chopped

MAKES 6–8 SERVINGS

Preheat the oven to 325°F (165°C). Place the meat on a plate, season lightly with salt and pepper, and dust evenly with the flour. In a 5½- to 7-qt (5.5- to 7-l) dutch oven over medium heat, warm 5 tablespoons (3 fl oz/ 80 ml) of the olive oil. Add the meat and cook until well browned, about 4 minutes per side. Transfer to a plate and set aside.

Add the garlic, onion, celery, and carrot to the pot and sauté until soft and golden brown, about 5 minutes. Add the thyme, oregano, bay leaf, and rosemary and and stir well. Return the meat to the pan. Pour in the broth and wine and bring to a boil. Remove from the heat and cover. Place in the oven and cook, turning the meat halfway through, for 2½ hours.

Just before the chuck roast is done, in a 10-inch (25-cm) frying pan over medium-high heat, warm the remaining 3 tablespoons olive oil. Add the chanterelles and sauté until golden brown, about 5 minutes. Remove from the heat and set aside.

Remove the meat from the oven and transfer to a plate. Strain the braising liquid through a fine-mesh sieve and return to the pot. Add the meat and the chanterelles and return to the oven. Cook until the meat is very tender, about 30 minutes.

Remove from the oven and turn the oven off. Transfer the meat and chanterelles to an ovenproof dish, tent with foil, and place in the oven.

Set the dutch oven over medium-high heat, bring the braising liquid to a boil, and cook until reduced by half, 8–10 minutes. Remove the meat from the oven and uncover. Pour the reduced sauce over and around the meat. Cut into slices and serve right away.

Slow braising in a cast-iron pot is a great way to cook large, tough pieces of meat and seasonal vegetables. Any mushroom variety can replace the chanterelles.

carnitas tacos

3½ lb (1.75 kg) boneless pork shoulder, cut into 2-inch (5-cm) pieces

Sea salt and cracked pepper

4 cloves garlic, unpeeled

2 jalapeño chiles, halved lengthwise

2 teaspoons ground cumin

1 lime, quartered, plus quarters for serving

1 bay leaf

4 cups (32 fl oz/1 l) chicken broth

Warmed flour tortillas, sour cream, hot sauce, chopped fresh cilantro, and tomatillo salsa for serving

MAKES 6–8 SERVINGS

Season the pork with salt and pepper. In a 5½- to 7-qt (5.5- to 7-l) dutch oven over medium heat, combine the pork, garlic, chiles, cumin, lime, and bay leaf. Pour in the broth and bring to a boil. Reduce the heat to low, cover, and simmer until the meat is fork-tender, about 4 hours.

Preheat the oven to 425°F (220°C). Using a slotted spoon, transfer the pork to a large baking dish; set the dutch oven aside. Using 2 forks, pull the pork apart into rough shreds. Place the dish in the oven and roast until the pork is crispy, about 20 minutes.

Meanwhile, place the dutch oven over medium-high heat, bring the cooking liquid to a boil, and cook, without stirring, until the liquid is reduced to about 1 cup (8 fl oz/250 ml), 15–20 minutes.

Remove the pork from the oven and transfer to a bowl. Strain the reduced sauce and pour over the pork. Serve right away with the tortillas, sour cream, hot sauce, lime quarters, cilantro, and salsa.

For *carnitas,* meaning "little meats," pork shoulder is very slowly braised in a spicy broth. Then it is shredded and roasted quickly in a hot oven. The finished meat, both juicy and crisp, is wrapped inside tortillas and garnished with salsa and other condiments.

garlic-braised chicken

1 chicken, about 3½ lb (1.75 kg), cut into 8 pieces

2 teaspoons herbes de Provence

Sea salt and cracked pepper

¼ cup (2 fl oz/60 ml) olive oil

40 cloves garlic, peeled

1½ cups (12 fl oz/375 ml) chicken broth

1 cup (8 fl oz/250 ml) dry white vermouth

¼ cup (2 fl oz/60 ml) Calvados or apple brandy

2 sprigs fresh thyme

½ cup (½ oz/15 g) fresh flat-leaf parsley leaves, torn

MAKES 4–6 SERVINGS

Place the chicken pieces in a bowl and toss with the herbes de Provence. Season lightly with salt and pepper, toss again, and set aside.

In a 5½- to 7-qt (5.5- to 7-l) dutch oven over medium-high heat, warm the olive oil. Working in batches, cook the seasoned chicken pieces until dark golden brown, about 5 minutes per side. Transfer to a plate.

Reduce the heat to medium, add the garlic to the pot, and sauté, stirring continuously, until deep golden brown, about 8 minutes.

Return the chicken to the pot and add the broth, vermouth, and Calvados. Top with the thyme sprigs and bring to a boil over medium-high heat. Reduce the heat to medium-low, cover, and simmer until the chicken is opaque throughout, about 30 minutes.

Transfer the chicken to a warmed serving dish and tent loosely with foil. Raise the heat to medium-high, bring the sauce to a boil, and cook until slightly reduced, about 5 minutes. Pour the sauce over the chicken and sprinkle with the parsley. Serve right away.

Simple to prepare, this chicken is layered with deep flavor. Although the quantity of garlic sounds like a lot, the cloves become sweet and nutty when braised in an aromatic broth that is later thickened into a sauce. Serve with crusty bread.

asian-style braised short ribs

3½ lb (1.75 kg)
beef short ribs

½ cup (4 fl oz/125 ml)
hoisin sauce

¼ cup (2 fl oz/60 ml)
soy sauce

¼ cup (2 fl oz/60 ml)
dry sherry

3 tablespoons honey

3 tablespoons
Asian sesame oil

2 tablespoons grated
fresh ginger

1 tablespoon Chinese
five-spice powder

1 tablespoon
Dijon mustard

4 star anise pods

2 cloves garlic,
finely chopped

1 red jalapeño chile,
finely chopped

1 bunch green onions,
thinly sliced

Fresh cilantro leaves
for garnish

MAKES 4–6 SERVINGS

Arrange the ribs in a single layer in a nonreactive dish. In a bowl, whisk together the hoisin sauce, soy sauce, sherry, honey, sesame oil, ginger, five-spice powder, mustard, star anise, garlic, and chile. Pour over the ribs and turn to coat well. Cover and marinate in the refrigerator for at least 4 hours or up to overnight.

Remove the ribs from the refrigerator and bring to room temperature. Preheat the oven to 350°F (180°C).

Place the ribs in a 5½- to 7-qt (5.5- to 7-l) braiser and pour the marinade over the top. Cover the pot and bake for 1 hour. Uncover and continue to cook for 30 minutes. Turn over the ribs and cook until the meat is very tender, the sauce has thickened, and the ribs are coated with a sticky brown glaze, about 30 minutes.

Remove from the oven, cover, and let stand for 5 minutes. Sprinkle the ribs with the green onions and cilantro and serve right away.

The sweet-and-spicy ribs are slowly braised in a dark, rich sauce of honey, toasted sesame oil, soy sauce, jalapeño, and fresh ginger. The tight-fitting lid and self-basting properties of the dutch oven allow the ribs to become succulent. You could also use a braiser.

or

coq au vin

1 chicken, about 3 lb (1.5 kg), cut into 8 pieces

Sea salt and cracked pepper

6 tablespoons (3 fl oz/ 90 ml) olive oil, or as needed

1 large yellow onion, chopped

4 cloves garlic, finely chopped

3 slices smoked bacon, roughly chopped

2 carrots, sliced

1 stalk celery, sliced

2 bay leaves

2 tablespoons herbes de Provence

3 cups (24 fl oz/750 ml) dry white wine

3 cups (24 fl oz/750 ml) chicken broth

1 cup (8 fl oz/250 ml) heavy cream

1 small bunch fresh tarragon, chopped

MAKES 4–6 SERVINGS

Season the chicken pieces with salt and pepper and set aside.

In a 5½- to 7-qt (5.5- to 7-l) dutch oven over medium heat, warm the olive oil. Add the onion, garlic, bacon, carrots, celery, bay leaves, and herbes de Provence. Sauté until all of the vegetables are soft and golden brown, 8–10 minutes. Transfer to a bowl and set aside.

Place the seasoned chicken pieces in the pot, adding more oil if the pot is dry. Cook, turning once with tongs, until the chicken is dark golden brown, about 5 minutes per side.

Return the onion mixture to the pot, pour in the wine and the broth, and bring to a boil. Reduce the heat to low, cover, and simmer, without stirring, until the chicken is opaque throughout and the juices have reduced slightly, about 45 minutes.

Remove from the heat and adjust the seasoning with salt and pepper. Let the stew stand, covered, for 5 minutes. Stir in the cream, sprinkle with the tarragon, and serve right away.

This version of a traditional French stew substitutes white wine for the typical red and adds cream for a rich, hearty dish. For an attractive presentation, bring the pot to the table and serve the chicken in large bowls. Accompany with a crusty baguette.

rustic walnut no-knead bread

3 cups (15 oz/470 g)
all-purpose flour, plus
flour for dusting

¼ teaspoon active
dry yeast

1¾ teaspoons
fine sea salt

1 cup (4 oz/125 g)
coarsely chopped
walnuts

Cornmeal as needed

MAKES 1 LOAF

In a large bowl, combine the 3 cups flour, yeast, salt, and walnuts. Add 1½ cups plus 2 tablespoons water and stir until blended; the dough will be shaggy and very sticky. Cover the bowl with plastic wrap. Let the dough rest at warm room temperature (about 70°F/21°C) until the surface is dotted with bubbles, 12–18 hours.

Turn the dough out onto a lightly floured work surface. Dust the dough with a little flour and fold the dough over itself once or twice. Cover loosely with plastic wrap and let rest for 15 minutes. Using just enough flour to keep the dough from sticking to the work surface or to your fingers, gently and quickly shape the dough into a ball. Generously coat a smooth cotton towel with cornmeal. Place the dough, seam side down, on the towel and dust with more flour or cornmeal. Cover with another towel and let the dough rise until it has more than doubled in bulk and does not readily spring back when poked with a finger, about 2 hours.

About 30 minutes before the dough is ready, place a dutch oven with a capacity of about 3 qt (3 l) in the oven and preheat to 450°F (230°C).

Remove the pot from the oven. Turn the dough, seam side up, into the pot; don't worry if the dough looks messy. Shake the pot once or twice to distribute the dough in the pot. Cover and bake for 30 minutes. Uncover and bake until the loaf is well browned, 15–30 minutes.

Transfer the pot to a wire rack and let cool for 10 minutes. Using oven mitts, turn the pot on its side and gently turn the bread out of the pot. It will release easily. Let cool slightly and cut into slices to serve.

This bread does not require kneading, but you must plan ahead: the dough needs to be prepared a day in advance. The trapped moisture in the tightly covered pot helps the bread develop an appealing crusty surface.

buttermilk doughnuts with lemon sugar

For the lemon sugar

½ cup (4 oz/125 g) evaporated cane sugar or granulated sugar

Finely grated zest of 2 Meyer lemons

2 cups (10 oz/315 g) all-purpose flour, plus flour for dusting

¾ cup (6 oz/185 g) evaporated cane sugar

2 teaspoons baking powder

1 teaspoon baking soda

Pinch sea salt

½ cup (4 fl oz/125 ml) buttermilk

1 large egg

2 tablespoons unsalted butter, melted

1 teaspoon vanilla extract

Canola oil for frying

MAKES 30 DOUGHNUTS

To make the lemon sugar, in a wide, shallow bowl, stir together the sugar and lemon zest until well mixed. Set aside.

In a food processor, combine the flour, sugar, baking powder, baking soda, and salt. Pulse briefly to blend. In a bowl, whisk together the buttermilk, egg, butter, and vanilla. With the motor running, add the wet ingredients to the dry ingredients and process until the dough forms a ball.

Transfer the dough to a floured work surface and roll out until 1 inch (2.5 cm) thick. Using a 1½-inch (4-cm) round pastry cutter, cut the dough into rounds. Knead the scraps, roll out, and cut more rounds.

Pour the oil to a depth of at least 3 inches (7.5 cm) into an dutch oven with at least a 5 qt (5 l) capacity. Heat over medium heat until the oil registers 350°F (180°C) on a deep-frying thermometer. Place a wire rack over a rimmed baking sheet and set near the stove.

Working in batches, carefully slide the doughnuts into the hot oil and cook, turning once with tongs, until dark golden brown, about 2 minutes per side. Adjust the heat if the doughnuts are turning brown too quickly. Transfer the doughnuts to the rack and let drain. Return the oil to 350°F before cooking the next batch.

Toss the warm doughnuts in the lemon sugar and serve right away.

Freshly made, bite-sized doughnuts rolled in sugar perfumed with Meyer lemon are divine. Evaporated cane sugar is sometimes labeled as "organic sugar" and resembles slightly coarser granulated sugar with an appealing light-caramel hue.

berry cobbler

3 cups (12 oz/375 g)
fresh raspberries

3 cups (12 oz/375 g)
fresh blackberries

⅔ cup (5 oz/155 g)
packed dark brown sugar

1 tablespoon
all-purpose flour

For the topping

1½ cups (7½ oz/235 g)
all-purpose flour

4 tablespoons (2 oz/60 g)
packed dark brown sugar

1 tablespoon baking
powder

1 teaspoon ground
ginger

Pinch sea salt

4 tablespoons (2 oz/60 g)
cold unsalted butter,
cut into cubes

1 cup (8 fl oz/250 ml)
heavy cream

1 lb (500 g) mascarpone
for serving

MAKES 6–8 SERVINGS

Preheat the oven to 375°F (190°C).

Place the berries in a bowl. Add the brown sugar and flour and toss well. Set the berry mixture aside.

To make the topping, in a food processor, combine the flour, 2 tablespoons of the brown sugar, the baking powder, ginger, and salt. Pulse to blend. Add the butter and pulse until the mixture resembles bread crumbs. With the motor running, pour in the cream until the mixture forms a dough.

Pour the berry mixture into a 3½- to 4-qt (3.5- to 4-l) dutch oven or braiser. Top the surface evenly with spoonfuls of the dough. Sprinkle the dough with the remaining 2 tablespoons brown sugar. Bake until the topping is golden brown and the berries are bubbling, 30–35 minutes.

Spoon the cobbler into bowls, top with mascarpone, and serve right away.

Here, two varieties of berries are topped with a brown sugar–ginger topping and baked in a dutch oven. Baking the dessert in an enameled pot makes a beautiful presentation if you bring it straight from the oven to the table for serving.

chocolate-raisin bread puddings

4 tablespoons (2 oz/60 g) salted butter, at room temperature

12 slices cinnamon-raisin bread

1 cup (8 fl oz/250 ml) heavy cream

1 cup (8 fl oz/250 ml) whole milk

8 oz (250 g) bittersweet chocolate, finely chopped

5 large eggs

¼ cup (2 oz/60 g) packed dark brown sugar, plus sugar for sprinkling

3 tablespoons dark rum

2 teaspoons vanilla extract

½ teaspoon ground cinnamon

Hot water

Cocoa powder for dusting

Crème fraîche for serving

MAKES 6 SERVINGS

Butter six 1-cup (8–fl oz/250-ml) dutch ovens and set aside.

Lay the bread slices on a work surface and butter them. Place 6 of the slices, buttered side up, on top of the remaining 6 slices. Cut each 2-slice stack from corner to corner into 4 triangles. Layer the triangles in the prepared dutch ovens.

In a saucepan over medium heat, warm the cream and milk until small bubbles appear around the edge of the pan. Remove from the heat and stir in the chocolate. Let stand until the chocolate is melted, about 4 minutes. Stir the mixture until smooth.

In a bowl, whisk together the eggs, ¼ cup sugar, rum, vanilla, and cinnamon. Add the warm chocolate mixture and whisk to mix thoroughly. Pour over the bread in the dutch ovens. Sprinkle each with a little brown sugar and cover with plastic wrap. Refrigerate until the bread soaks up the chocolate mixture, at least 1 hour or up to overnight.

Preheat the oven to 350°F (180°C). Place the dutch ovens in a 9-by-13-inch (23-by-33-cm) roasting pan. Pour in enough hot water to reach halfway up the sides of the dutch ovens. Place the pan in the oven and bake until the puddings are crisp on top and the custard has set, about 30 minutes.

Remove from the oven, dust the puddings with cocoa powder, and serve right away with crème fraîche.

This grown-up version of a childhood favorite combines cinnamon-raisin bread and a chocolate-infused custard. Baked in tiny dutch ovens, the puddings can be served straight from the oven as individual portions.

frying pans

Also called skillets, frying pans have broad bases and sides that flare outward, making them useful for cooking foods that must be turned, stirred often, or slid from the pan. They are primarily designed for cooking foods quickly in a small amount of hot fat to create crisp edges and golden, caramelized surfaces on foods such as fritters, skillet breads, or pork chops. Since cast-iron frying pans have metal handles, and can withstand high heat, they can also be used successfully in the oven to double as a baking or roasting pan.

tomato, arugula & goat cheese frittata

6 large eggs

½ cup (4 fl oz/125 ml) heavy cream

½ cup (4 fl oz/125 ml) whole milk

Sea salt and cracked pepper

4 oz (125 g) soft goat cheese, crumbled

¼ cup (2 fl oz/60 ml) olive oil

1 clove garlic, finely chopped

2 cups (12 oz/375 g) cherry tomatoes, halved

4 cups (4 oz/125 g) arugula, roughly chopped, plus ½ cup (½ oz/15 g) leaves for garnish

Extra-virgin olive oil for drizzling

MAKES 4–6 SERVINGS

Preheat the oven to 375°F (190°C).

In a bowl, whisk together the eggs, cream, and milk until smooth. Season lightly with salt and pepper. Add the cheese and stir once. Set aside.

In a 10-inch (25-cm) frying pan over medium heat, warm the ¼ cup olive oil. Add the garlic and sauté until light golden, about 1 minute. Add the tomatoes and sauté until slightly softened, about 3 minutes. Add the 4 cups chopped arugula and stir to mix.

Pour the egg mixture over the vegetables and cook until the mixture begins to set, about 5 minutes. Place in the oven and bake until the frittata has completely set and is golden brown on top, about 15 minutes. Remove from the oven and let stand for 5 minutes.

Sprinkle the frittata with the arugula leaves and drizzle with oil. Cut into wedges and serve right away.

Frittatas are versatile dishes and can be served for breakfast, lunch, or dinner. They are quick and easy to make and can be brought to the table in the pan. This frittata features sweet cherry tomatoes, peppery arugula, and tangy goat cheese.

dutch baby with cinnamon pears

4 tablespoons (2 oz/60 g)
unsalted butter

2 Bosc or Anjou pears,
cored and sliced

½ teaspoon ground
cinnamon

4 large eggs

¾ cup (6 fl oz/180 ml)
whole milk

1 teaspoon vanilla
extract

¾ cup (4 oz/125 g)
all-purpose flour

3 tablespoons packed
light brown sugar

Honey for serving

Confectioners' sugar
for serving

MAKES 6 SERVINGS

Preheat the oven to 450°F (230°C).

In a 10-inch (25-cm) frying pan over medium-high heat, melt the butter. Add the pears and cinnamon and cook, turning once, until the pears are golden brown, 3–4 minutes.

In a large bowl, using an electric mixer on medium speed, beat the eggs, milk, and vanilla until smooth. Continuing to beat on medium speed, slowly add the flour and then the sugar and beat until a smooth batter forms. Pour the batter over the pears. Bake until the pancake is puffed and golden brown, 12–15 minutes.

Remove from the oven and drizzle with honey. Dust with confectioners' sugar. Serve right away.

This sweet treat, ideal for a weekend brunch, can go straight from the oven to the table in the frying pan. Filled with luscious caramelized pears, it has a texture between that of a pancake and that of a popover.

zucchini fritters with herbed yogurt

For the herbed yogurt

1½ cups (12 oz/375 g) Greek yogurt

1 clove garlic, crushed and finely chopped

½ cup (¾ oz/20 g) chopped fresh mint

Sea salt and white pepper

Ground sumac for sprinkling (optional)

Extra-virgin olive oil for drizzling

½ cup (2½ oz/75 g) all-purpose flour

2 large eggs

2 tablespoons whole milk

Finely grated zest and juice of 1 lemon, plus 2 lemons, cut into wedges, for serving

Sea salt and white pepper

4 zucchini, shredded

1 clove garlic, crushed and finely chopped

¼ cup (⅓ oz/10 g) chopped fresh flat-leaf parsley

¼ cup (⅓ oz/10 g) chopped fresh mint

4 tablespoons (2 fl oz/ 60 ml) olive oil

MAKES 12–14 FRITTERS

To make the yogurt sauce, in a bowl, stir together the yogurt, garlic, and mint. Season with salt and pepper. Sprinkle with sumac, if using, and drizzle with extra-virgin olive oil. Cover and refrigerate until serving.

In a large bowl, whisk together the flour, eggs, milk, and lemon zest and juice. Season lightly with salt and pepper. Add the zucchini, garlic, parsley, and mint and stir until well combined.

In a 10-inch (25-cm) frying pan over medium-high heat, warm 2 tablespoons of the olive oil. Drop large tablespoons of the zucchini mixture into the pan. Cook until the bottoms are dark golden brown, about 3 minutes. Turn the fritters, reduce the heat to medium, and cook until dark golden brown on the second side, 3–4 minutes. Transfer to a serving plate. Cook additional fritters, using the remaining 2 tablespoons olive oil.

Serve the fritters right away with the yogurt sauce and lemon wedges.

Mediterranean-style zucchini fritters cook to a golden brown finish in a cast-iron pan. They are delicious dipped into a simple yogurt sauce. Ground sumac is a lemony spice used in Middle Eastern cooking. Look for it at Middle Eastern or specialty food markets.

jalapeño-cheddar corn bread

1 tablespoon
unsalted butter

1 cup (5 oz/155 g)
all-purpose flour

1 cup (5 oz/155 g)
cornmeal

2 tablespoons packed
light brown sugar

1 tablespoon
baking powder

½ teaspoon sea salt

3 large eggs

1 cup (8 fl oz/250 ml)
whole milk

¼ cup (2 fl oz/60 ml)
olive oil

1 cup (6 oz/185)
fresh or thawed,
frozen corn kernels

2 jalapeño chiles, seeded
and finely chopped

1½ cups (6 oz/185 g)
shredded sharp Cheddar
cheese

MAKES 6–8 SERVINGS

Preheat the oven to 350°F (180°C). Coat a 10-inch (25-cm) frying pan
with the butter. Set aside.

In a large bowl, combine the flour, cornmeal, sugar, baking powder, and
salt. In another bowl, whisk together the eggs, milk, and olive oil. Pour the
egg mixture into the flour mixture and stir to blend. Add the corn kernels,
the chiles, and 1 cup (4 oz/125 g) of the cheese and stir to combine.

Pour the batter into the prepared frying pan and sprinkle with the
remaining cheese. Bake until the bread has risen and is golden on top,
25–30 minutes. Remove from the oven and let cool in the pan for
5 minutes. Cut into wedges and serve right away.

Baking corn bread in a seasoned cast iron frying pan
helps develop a deeply golden crust. This Mexican-inspired
version is enlivened with spicy chiles, sharp Cheddar
cheese, and sweet corn kernels.

easy paella with shrimp & chorizo

4 tablespoons
(2 fl oz/60 ml) olive oil

15 medium shrimp,
shells intact

2 Spanish-style cured
chorizo sausages, sliced

2 cloves garlic,
finely chopped

1 yellow onion,
finely chopped

4 tomatoes, chopped

2 jarred piquillo peppers
or 1 roasted red bell
pepper, chopped

1½ teaspoons Spanish
smoked sweet paprika
or regular sweet paprika

1½ cups (12 fl oz/375 ml)
chicken broth

½ teaspoon saffron
threads soaked in
¼ cup (2 fl oz/60 ml)
dry white wine

1½ cups (10½ oz/330 g)
paella rice (see Note)

1 cup (1 oz/30 g)
fresh flat-leaf parsley
leaves, torn

6–8 lemon wedges

MAKES 6–8 SERVINGS

In a 10-inch (25-cm) frying pan over medium-high heat, warm 2 tablespoons of the olive oil. Add the shrimp and sauté until pink, 3–5 minutes. Transfer to a bowl and set aside. Add the chorizo to the pan and cook until brown and crispy, 4–5 minutes. Transfer to the bowl with the shrimp.

Add the remaining 2 tablespoons oil to the pan. Add the garlic and onion and sauté until soft and golden brown, 3–4 minutes. Add the tomatoes, peppers, and paprika. Cook, stirring frequently, until the mixture has thickened and most of the liquid has evaporated, about 5 minutes.

In a small saucepan, bring the broth and saffron mixture to a boil. Reduce the heat to maintain a simmer.

Stir the rice into the tomato mixture and cook for 2 minutes. Pour the simmering broth mixture over the rice, stir well, and bring to a boil. Reduce the heat to medium-low and simmer without stirring until the liquid is absorbed by the rice, 8–10 minutes.

Add the shrimp and chorizo and push them down into the rice. Cover the pan with foil and cook until the shrimp and chorizo are cooked through and the rice is cooked, about 10 minutes. Turn off the heat and let the paella stand for 5 minutes. Remove the foil and sprinkle with chopped parsley. Garnish with the lemon wedges and serve right away.

A taste of Spain in a single pan, paella is a delicious dish to prepare for company. Saffron, tomatoes, and pink shrimp make it a feast for the eyes as well. Look for Spanish paella rice such as Bomba or any rice variety from Spain's Valencia region in a specialty-food store.

cider-glazed pork chops with figs

4 bone-in, center-cut
pork chops, each about
1-inch (2.5-cm) thick

Sea salt and cracked
pepper

12 dried figs or 6 fresh
figs, quartered

3 tablespoons olive oil

1 clove garlic,
finely chopped

2 shallots, finely chopped

3 tablespoons fresh
thyme leaves

⅓ cup (3 oz/90 g)
good-quality fig jam

1 cup (8 fl oz/250 ml)
apple cider

MAKES 4 SERVINGS

Season the chops lightly with salt and pepper. Set aside. If using dried figs, soak them in warm water for 30 minutes to rehydrate. Drain well.

In a 10-inch (25-cm) frying pan over medium-high heat, warm the olive oil. Add the garlic, shallots, and thyme and sauté until the vegetables are golden brown, about 3 minutes.

Add the pork chops to the pan and cook, turning once, until well browned on each side, about 5 minutes per side. Transfer the pork chops to a plate, tent with foil, and keep warm.

Add the jam to the juices in the pan and cook, stirring, until the jam is melted. Add the cider and bring to a boil. Reduce the heat to medium and return the chops to the pan. Add the figs. Cook, turning the chops once, until golden brown and the meat is cooked to your liking, about 5 minutes for medium. Turn off the heat, loosely cover the pan with foil, and let the meat rest for 5 minutes. Serve right away.

Searing the pork chops first in a hot cast-iron pan gives them a beautiful golden brown color. They finish cooking in a mixture of cider and fig jam. Figs, fresh or dried, complete this autumn feast.

maple tarte tatin

9-inch (23-cm) square
frozen puff pastry,
thawed

Flour for dusting

4 Granny Smith apples

2 tablespoons butter

2 tablespoons
maple syrup

½ cup (4 oz/125 g) sugar

Vanilla ice cream
for serving

MAKES 6 SERVINGS

Preheat the oven to 400°F (200°C). Lay the pastry on a lightly floured work surface and roll out to roughly fit the diameter of a 10-inch (25-cm) frying pan. Core the apples, cut them in half, and thinly slice.

In the frying pan over medium-high heat, melt the butter with the maple syrup. Add the sugar and cook, stirring, until the sugar has melted and the mixture looks syrupy, 2–3 minutes. Continue to cook until the syrup turns golden brown, about 5 minutes.

Remove from the heat and arrange the apple slices in circles on the bottom of the pan, overlapping the slices as needed. Return the pan to medium-high heat and cook the apples until they are soft but still hold their shape and are golden brown, about 5 minutes.

Turn off the heat, place the pastry over the apples, and tuck the edges of the pastry down around the sides of the pan.

Bake until the pastry is golden brown and puffed up, about 20 minutes. Remove from the oven and let stand for 2 minutes. Invert the tart onto a serving plate, cut into wedges, and serve right away with vanilla ice cream.

In this version of a classic French dessert, apples are first caramelized in a cast-iron pan and then topped with puff pastry and baked to a golden finish. The apples are left unpeeled, which adds a contrasting color and texture to the dessert. Peel them if you wish.

grill pans

Stove-top grill pans feature prominent ridges across their cooking surface, which deliver nicely browned marks resembling those from the rack of an outdoor grill. The high temperature capabilities of cast iron ensure fast and even searing, leaving fish moist, steaks juicy at the center, and fruit caramelized. Some grill pans come with a special accessory called a *mattone*, or a panini press, that acts as a weight to encourage crisp skin on grilled chicken or crunchy crusts on sandwiches. These pans also have the advantage of draining off some of the fat from cooking food.

summer vegetables with balsamic

2 yellow summer
squash, sliced

2 zucchini, sliced

2 large portobello
mushroom caps, sliced

1 red bell pepper,
seeded and thickly sliced

1 orange bell pepper,
seeded and thickly sliced

1 yellow bell pepper,
seeded and thickly sliced

1 eggplant, sliced

1 cup (8 fl oz/250 ml)
olive oil, plus oil for
drizzling

½ cup (½ oz/15 g)
fresh marjoram leaves

½ cup (½ oz/15 g)
fresh oregano leaves

1 small bunch cherry
tomatoes on the vine,
or 1½ cups (9 oz/280 g)
small cherry tomatoes

Balsamic vinegar
for drizzling

Coarse sea salt and
cracked pepper

MAKES 6 SERVINGS

In a large bowl, combine the summer squash, zucchini, mushrooms, bell peppers, and eggplant. Add the 1 cup olive oil, marjoram, and oregano and toss well. Place the tomatoes on a plate and drizzle with oil.

Warm a grill pan over medium-high heat. Have ready a large platter for the grilled vegetables.

When the pan just begins to smoke, cook the vegetables in batches: add the tomatoes to the grill pan and cook, turning occasionally with tongs, until the skins are scorched and slightly blackened in places, about 4 minutes. Transfer to the platter.

Add the bell peppers and grill until charred and tender when pierced with a small knife, about 2 minutes per side. Transfer to the platter. Continue in the same manner to cook the zucchini and summer squash for 2 minutes per side, the eggplant for 3 minutes per side, and the mushrooms for 3–4 minutes per side.

Drizzle the grilled vegetables with balsamic vinegar, sprinkle generously with salt and pepper, and serve warm or at room temperature.

Quickly cooking fresh summer vegetables on a hot cast-iron grill pan helps retain their distinctive flavors and textures. Here, fragrant fresh herbs and a drizzle of tart-sweet vinegar mingle with the vegetable juices to form a simple sauce.

asparagus with tapenade

For the tapenade

1 cup (5 oz/155 g) pitted Kalamata olives

4 oil-packed anchovy fillets

½ cup (¾ oz/20 g) chopped fresh flat-leaf parsley

1 clove garlic

1 tablespoon salted capers

1 tablespoon fresh lemon juice

¼ cup (2 fl oz/60 ml) olive oil

1½ lb (750 g) thin asparagus spears, ends trimmed

¼ cup (2 fl oz/60 ml) olive oil

2 cloves garlic, crushed and finely chopped

Sea salt and cracked pepper

MAKES 4–6 SERVINGS

To make the tapenade, in a food processor, combine the olives, anchovies, parsley, garlic, capers, and lemon juice. With the motor running, add the olive oil in a thin, steady stream and process until a chunky paste forms. Spoon into a small serving bowl.

Warm the grill pan over medium-high heat. Meanwhile, in a glass dish, toss the asparagus with the olive oil and garlic. Season with salt and pepper.

When the pan just begins to smoke, add the asparagus and grill, turning once, until the spears are tender and well browned, 6–9 minutes total. Transfer to a serving plate.

Serve right away with the tapenade for dipping.

Pan-grilling asparagus brings out its natural nutty qualities and mellows its assertive edge. At a dinner party, accompany it with this provençal olive dip for a simple finger food or an antipasto.

fish tacos with mango salsa

4 tilapia fillets, about
2 lb (1 kg) total weight

Grated zest and juice
of 2 limes

3 tablespoons olive oil

1 red jalapeño chile,
seeded and minced

½ cup (¾ oz/20 g) fresh
cilantro leaves, torn

Sea salt and cracked
pepper

8 flour tortillas

For the mango salsa

1 mango, peeled
and finely chopped

1 serrano chile, seeded
and finely chopped

¼ cup (1 oz/30 g) finely
chopped red bell pepper

¼ cup (⅓ oz/10 g)
fresh cilantro leaves

Juice of 1 lime

3 tablespoons olive oil

4 limes, quartered,
for serving

Hot sauce for serving

MAKES 4 SERVINGS

Lay the fish fillets in a single layer in a nonreactive baking dish. In a bowl, whisk together the lime zest and juice, olive oil, jalapeño, and cilantro and pour over the fish. Season lightly with salt and pepper. Cover the dish and set aside for 10 minutes.

Preheat the oven to 350°F (180°C).

Wrap the tortillas in foil and place in the oven. Meanwhile, to make the salsa, in a bowl, mix together the mango, chile, bell pepper, and cilantro. Add the lime juice and olive oil and toss well. Set aside.

Warm a grill pan over medium-high heat. When the pan just begins to smoke, lay the fish in the pan and reduce the heat to medium. Cook, turning once, until the fish is opaque throughout, about 3 minutes per side. Transfer to a warmed large serving plate.

Remove the tortillas from the oven and place alongside the fish. Serve at once with the mango salsa, lime wedges, and hot sauce.

Tilapia fillets, marinated briefly in lime juice and chile, cook in just minutes in a stove-top grill pan. The fresh mango salsa comes together easily, making for a quick meal. For even faster assembly, use purchased salsa.

lamb chops with garlic & thyme

1 rack of lamb, 1½–2 lb (750 g–1 kg), cut into 8 chops

¾ cup (6 fl oz/180 ml) olive oil

3 tablespoons lemon thyme leaves

3 cloves garlic, crushed and finely chopped

Sea salt and cracked pepper

MAKES 2–3 SERVINGS

Place the chops in a single layer in a nonreactive dish. In a small bowl, mix together the olive oil, thyme, and garlic. Pour the oil mixture over the chops and rub it on both sides of the meat. Season with salt and pepper. Cover and let stand for about 30 minutes.

Warm a grill pan over medium-high heat. When the pan just begins to smoke, add the chops to the pan and cook until the meat is well browned, 2–3 minutes per side. Turn off the heat, tent the meat with foil, and let stand for about 4 minutes. Serve right away.

There are several varieties of fragrant thyme. Lemon thyme, used here, brings out the flavors of the lamb and garlic. The lamb takes little time to prepare, making it a convenient and elegant dish for a busy weeknight.

rib eye steaks with onion marmalade

For the onion marmalade

3 tablespoons olive oil

2 red onions, thinly sliced

⅓ cup (4 oz/125 g) maple syrup

1 tablespoon fresh rosemary leaves

1 tablespoon balsamic vinegar

1 tablespoon red pepper flakes

Sea salt and cracked pepper

4 rib eye steaks, each about 8 oz (250 g) and 1 inch (2.5 cm) thick

¼ cup (2 fl oz/60 ml) olive oil

Sea salt and cracked pepper

MAKES 4 SERVINGS

To make the onion marmalade, in a 10-inch (25-cm) frying pan over medium heat, warm the olive oil. Add the onions, maple syrup, rosemary, vinegar, and pepper flakes and stir to coat the onions well. Season with salt and pepper. Reduce the heat to low and simmer, stirring occasionally, until the onions are soft and have absorbed all the liquid, about 30 minutes.

Meanwhile, warm a grill pan over medium-high heat. Lay the steaks on a plate, drizzle both sides with the oil, and season with salt and pepper.

When the pan just begins to smoke, add the steaks and cook until the meat is well browned, about 4 minutes. Turn the steaks and cook for 4 minutes longer for medium rare or until cooked to your liking.

Turn off the heat and loosely cover the pan with foil. Let the meat rest for 10 minutes to redistribute the juices.

Slice the steaks and serve right away with the onion marmalade.

Thick onion marmalade, spiked with red pepper flakes to offset its sweetness, makes a tempting sweet-spicy partner for juicy pan-grilled steaks. Any remaining marmalade can be spread on sandwiches or served with other pan-grilled meats.

chicken under a brick

1 chicken, 3½–4 lb
(1.75–2 kg), butterflied
and backbone removed

Sea salt and cracked
pepper

¼ cup (⅓ oz/10 g)
fresh thyme leaves

¼ cup (⅓ oz/10 g)
fresh rosemary leaves

¼ cup (⅓ oz/10 g)
fresh marjoram leaves

Grated zest and juice
of 1 lemon, plus 1 lemon,
sliced

¼ cup (2 fl oz/60 ml)
olive oil

MAKES 4–6 SERVINGS

Lay the chicken flat on a work surface and season generously on both sides with salt and pepper.

In a small bowl, mix together the thyme, rosemary, marjoram, lemon zest and lemon juice, and olive oil. Season lightly with salt and pepper.

Carefully insert the lemon slices under the skin of the chicken and rub the chicken all over with the herbed olive oil mixture.

Preheat the oven 375°F (190°C). Warm a grill pan over medium-high heat. If you do not have a *mattone* (see page 70), wrap a brick in foil or use a cast-iron frying pan to weight the chicken.

When the pan just begins to smoke, place the chicken skin side down in the pan and immediately top with the *mattone,* foil-covered brick, or frying pan. Reduce the heat to medium and cook the chicken until the skin is crisp and brown, about 20 minutes. Remove the pan from the heat and remove the weight. Turn the chicken over and replace the weight.

Transfer the weighted chicken to the oven and roast until an instant-read thermometer inserted into the thickest part of the breast reads 170°F (77°C), about 20 minutes. Remove from the oven and remove the weight. Loosely cover the chicken with foil and let stand for 10 minutes.

Cut into serving pieces, and transfer to a warmed platter. Serve right away, drizzled with the juices from the pan.

Pollo al mattone is a Tuscan way of grilling chicken under a heavy weight so that the skin becomes very crisp and the meat tender. To save time, ask the butcher to butterfly the chicken—that is, remove the backbone and flatten the bird.

three-cheese panini

8 slices rustic rosemary bread, each about ½ inch (12 mm) thick

¾ cup (6 fl oz/180 ml) olive oil

Dijon mustard

4 oz (125 g) fontina cheese, sliced

4 oz (125 g) Manchego cheese, sliced

4 oz (125 g) sharp Cheddar cheese, sliced

2 cups (2 oz/60 g) arugula leaves

Cracked pepper

MAKES 4 SERVINGS

Place the bread slices on a baking sheet and brush both sides generously with the olive oil. Spread 4 slices with a thin layer of mustard. Layer the sliced cheeses on top of the mustard, dividing them evenly. Top the cheese with the arugula, dividing it evenly, and season with pepper. Top with the remaining 4 slices of bread.

Warm a grill pan over medium-high heat. When the pan just begins to smoke, place 2 sandwiches in the pan and weight with a stove-top panini press, *mattone* (see page 70), or heavy pot lid. Grill the sandwiches until golden and crispy, about 2 minutes. Remove the weight, turn the sandwiches, replace the weight, and grill until golden and crispy on the second side, about 2 minutes longer. Repeat with remaining sandwiches. Serve right away.

Panini are Italian grilled sandwiches made with thick rustic bread and savory fillings. They are cooked on a grill pan with a weight placed on top. The filling ingredients meld together, and the bread toasts and becomes crunchy to the bite.

peaches with cardamom honey

6 ripe yellow or white peaches, halved and pitted

1 tablespoon unsalted butter, melted

12 tablespoons (6 fl oz/ 180 ml) honey

Ground cardamom for sprinkling

1½ cups (12 oz/375 g) crème fraîche for serving

MAKES 6 SERVINGS

Warm a grill pan over high heat. Meanwhile, lay the peach halves cut side up on a work surface and brush with the melted butter.

When the pan just begins to smoke, place the buttered peaches cut side down in the pan and cook until they start to release their juices and turn golden brown, about 3 minutes. Turn the peaches and reduce the heat to medium-low. Fill each peach half with 1 tablespoon honey and sprinkle lightly with cardamom. Cook until the peaches soften but still hold their shape, 5–6 minutes longer. Serve right away with dollops of crème fraîche.

Grilling peaches in a cast-iron pan intensifies their natural sweetness and lends a faintly smoky flavor to the fruit. As the peaches cook, they are drizzled with honey and sprinkled with cardamom. When the honey melts, it infuses the fruit with spice.

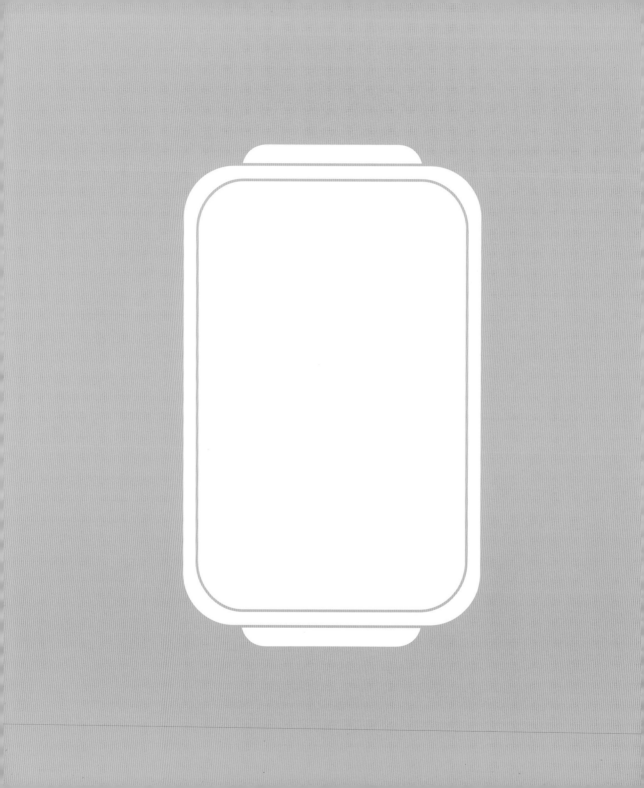

baking, roasting & gratin pans

Used for baking both savory and sweet foods, these ovenproof pans come in a variety of shapes and sizes. Roasting pans are generally large and rectangular in shape with low, straight sides. Their form allows the oven's heat to reach as much of the food as possible to achieve golden brown surfaces on large cuts of meat or pronounced caramelization on root vegetables. Rectangular baking pans hold casseroles and layered pastas, contributing to nicely melted cheeses and evenly bubbling sauces. Oval or round gratin pans feature low, sloping sides to encourage crisp, golden brown crusts, perfect for bread crumb toppings or the brown sugar-and-oats coating on a fruit crisp.

breakfast strata

Butter for greasing

2 tablespoons olive oil

6 slices smoked bacon, chopped

2 Yukon gold potatoes, peeled and finely chopped

½ yellow onion, finely chopped

1 portobello mushroom cap, finely chopped

1 tablespoon finely chopped fresh sage

3 cups (6 oz/185 g) baguette cubes (about ½-inch/12-mm cubes)

9 large eggs

3 cups (24 fl oz/750 ml) whole milk

Sea salt and cracked pepper

1½ cups (6 oz/185 g) shredded mozzarella cheese

1 cup (1½ oz/45 g) chopped fresh flat-leaf parsley

MAKES 6 SERVINGS

Butter a 9-by-13-inch (23-by-33-cm) pan.

Warm a 10-inch (25-cm) frying pan over medium-high heat and add the olive oil. Add the bacon, potatoes, and onion and sauté until the potatoes and onions are golden brown, about 5 minutes. Add the mushroom and sage and cook until softened, about 2 minutes. Remove from the heat and stir in the bread cubes. Transfer the mixture to the prepared pan.

In a bowl, whisk together eggs and milk. Season lightly with salt and pepper, and stir in the cheese and parsley. Pour over the bread mixture in the pan. Cover with plastic wrap and refrigerate for at least 30 minutes or preferably overnight.

Preheat the oven to 350°F (180°C). About 20 minutes before baking the strata, remove it from the refrigerator.

Bake until the strata has puffed up, the eggs have set, and the top is golden brown, 50–55 minutes. Serve right away.

This is a delicious, no-stress breakfast dish. You can prepare it the night before and refrigerate it overnight. The next day, there is nothing to do except bake the strata, letting you relax and enjoy your morning coffee.

potato & chard gratin

Butter for greasing

2 tablespoons olive oil

1 bunch rainbow
chard, about 1 lb (500 g),
leaves and tender stems
thinly sliced

1 clove garlic,
finely chopped

2 lb (1 kg) potatoes, sliced
wafer-thin, preferably
with a mandoline

4 oz (125 g) fontina
cheese, shredded

1½ cups (12 fl oz/375 ml)
heavy cream

Sea salt and cracked
pepper

½ cup (2 oz/60 g) freshly
grated Parmesan cheese

MAKES 4–6 SERVINGS

Preheat the oven to 375°F (190°C). Butter a 2-qt (2-l) gratin dish.

In a 10-inch (25-cm) frying pan over medium-high heat, warm the olive oil.
Add the chard and garlic and cook until the chard is slightly wilted, about
2 minutes. Remove from the heat.

Layer half of the potatoes, overlapping slightly if needed, in the prepared
dish. Layer half of the chard on top and sprinkle with half of the fontina
cheese. Repeat each layer, using the remaining potatoes, chard, and
fontina. Place the cream in a bowl, season generously with salt and pepper,
and stir well. Pour evenly over the potatoes and chard. Sprinkle the top
evenly with the Parmesan cheese.

Cover the dish tightly with foil and bake for about 30 minutes. Remove
the foil and bake until the top of the gratin is golden and crisp, about
15 minutes. Serve right away.

Gratins are quick to assemble before they are baked.
Here, chard in a rainbow of hues is paired with sliced
potatoes to create contrasting flavors and textures.
You can vary the gratin by using an array of potatoes,
such as red, purple, or white.

roasted root vegetables

3 beets, peeled
and quartered

⅓ cup (3 fl oz/80 ml)
olive oil

6 carrots, cut lengthwise
into quarters

6 potatoes, quartered

6 cloves garlic

3 parsnips, peeled
and cut lengthwise
into quarters

¼ cup (⅓ oz/10 g)
fresh marjoram leaves

¼ cup (⅓ oz/10 g)
fresh oregano leaves

2 sprigs fresh thyme

1 sprig fresh rosemary

Coarse sea salt and
cracked pepper

Balsamic vinegar
for drizzling

MAKES 4–6 SERVINGS

Preheat the oven to 375°F (190°C). Place the beets in a small bowl and toss with a little of the olive oil. Combine the carrots, potatoes, garlic, parsnips, marjoram, oregano, thyme, and rosemary in a 9-by-13-inch (23-by-33-cm) pan. Drizzle with the remaining olive oil and toss well. Add the beets and season all the vegetables generously with pepper. Drizzle with a little balsamic vinegar.

Roast the vegetables until dark golden brown, crisp around the edges, and tender when pierced with a small knife, about 35 minutes. Remove from the oven, sprinkle lightly with salt, and serve right away.

Roasting seals in the sweetness and robust flavors of root vegetables. Be sure to cut them to the same thickness so they are all done at the same time. The beets are added separately so that they don't impart too much color to the mixture. You can also use golden beets.

macaroni & cheese with bread crumbs

Butter for greasing

Sea salt and cracked pepper

1 lb (500 g) large elbow macaroni

2 large eggs

2 cups (16 fl oz/500 ml) whole milk

1 cup (8 fl oz/250 ml) heavy cream

2 cloves garlic, finely chopped

½ lb (250 g) Gruyère cheese, shredded

½ lb (250 g) Emmentaler cheese, shredded

2 cups (4 oz/125 g) fresh bread crumbs

Extra-virgin olive oil for drizzling

Truffle oil for serving (optional)

MAKES 6–8 SERVINGS

Preheat the oven to 375°F (190°C). Butter a 1½- to 2-quart (1.5- to 2-l) oval gratin pan or a 9-by-13-inch (23-by-33-cm) baking pan.

Bring a large pot of water to a boil. Add a pinch of salt and the macaroni, stir, and cook until almost cooked, about 5 minutes. Drain, rinse, drain again, and set aside.

In a large bowl, whisk together the eggs, milk, cream, and garlic. Season with salt and pepper. In another bowl, stir together the shredded Gruyère and Emmentaler cheeses.

Evenly sprinkle a third of the cheese in the prepared pan. Add half of the macaroni. Repeat the layers, ending with a layer of cheese. Pour the egg-milk mixture evenly over the top. Sprinkle the bread crumbs over the top and drizzle with olive oil.

Bake until the macaroni is bubbling and the top is dark golden brown, 40–45 minutes. Remove from the oven and drizzle with the truffle oil, if using. Serve right away.

Using a custard rather than a white sauce makes this version of macaroni & cheese both light and quick to prepare. The layers of tender macaroni and two flavorful cheeses are finished with a crunchy crumb topping and, before serving, with a drizzle of truffle oil.

96

or

cauliflower gratin

4 tablespoons (2 oz/60 g) butter, plus butter for greasing

1 head cauliflower, 2½–3 lb (1.25–1.5 kg)

Sea salt and white pepper

1 cup (8 fl oz/250 ml) heavy cream

1 cup (8 fl oz/250 ml) whole milk

4 tablespoons (1½ oz/ 45 g) all-purpose flour

1¾ cups (7 oz/220 g) shredded sharp white Cheddar cheese

2 teaspoons Dijon mustard

Freshly grated nutmeg

MAKES 4 SERVINGS

Preheat the oven to 375°F (190°C). Butter four 6½-inch (16.5-cm) frying pans or gratin dishes.

Bring a pot of water to a boil. Cut the cauliflower into florets. Add a pinch of salt and the cauliflower to the boiling water and cook until tender-crisp, 4–5 minutes. Drain, rinse with cold water, and drain again. Divide the cauliflower among the prepared dishes.

In a small saucepan over medium heat, warm the cream and milk until small bubbles appear around the edge of the pan. In a saucepan over medium heat, melt the 4 tablespoons butter. Stir in the flour and cook, stirring, for about 2 minutes. Whisking continuously, slowly add the warm cream mixture and cook until the sauce is thick and creamy, about 5 minutes.

Add the cheese and stir until it melts. Stir in the Dijon and season with salt and pepper. Pour the cheese sauce over the cauliflower, dividing it evenly. Sprinkle lightly with nutmeg.

Bake until the cheese sauce is bubbling and the top is golden brown, 15–20 minutes. Remove from the oven and serve right way.

or

or

Baked in individual frying pans or gratin dishes, this cauliflower can be served as a meatless main course or as a side dish for roasted meats or poultry. The nutmeg subtly perfumes the sharp cheese sauce. You can adjust the tanginess by using a spicier mustard.

meat lasagna

3 tablespoons olive oil, plus oil for greasing and drizzling

3 cloves garlic, minced

2 portobello mushroom caps, finely chopped

½ red onion, minced

1 tablespoon dried herbes de Provence

2 lb (1 kg) lean ground beef

1 cup (8 fl oz/250 ml) dry red wine

2 tablespoons sun-dried tomatoes, finely chopped

2 tablespoons tomato paste

Sea salt and cracked pepper

2 cans (28 oz/875 g each) diced tomatoes

1 lb (500 g) fresh lasagna noodles (about 9 sheets)

15 oz (470 g) fresh whole-milk ricotta

1 cup (4 oz/125 g) shredded mozzarella cheese

½ cup (2 oz/60 g) grated Parmesan cheese

1 cup (1 oz/30 g) fresh flat-leaf parsley leaves

MAKES 8–10 SERVINGS

First, make a meat sauce: In a 10-inch (25-cm) frying pan over medium-high heat, warm the 3 tablespoons olive oil. Add the garlic, mushrooms, onion, and herbes de Provence and sauté until the onion and garlic are soft and golden brown, 4–5 minutes.

Add the ground beef and cook, stirring and breaking up any large pieces with a wooden spoon, until browned, 6–8 minutes. Add the wine, sun-dried tomatoes, and tomato paste and stir well. Season lightly with salt and pepper. Simmer, stirring occasionally, until the meat is cooked through, about 15 minutes.

Meanwhile, preheat the oven to 350°F (180°C). Oil a 10-by-16-inch (25-by-40-cm) pan.

Spoon a third of the diced tomatoes into the prepared pan and spread in an even layer. Top with 3 sheets of lasagna noodles. Spoon half of the meat sauce over the top and spread evenly, and dot with a third of the ricotta. Repeat the layers of lasagna noodles, meat sauce, and ricotta. Top with the remaining lasagna noodles, diced tomatoes, and ricotta. Top with the mozzarella and Parmesan and drizzle with olive oil.

Bake until the lasagna is bubbling and brown on top, about 45 minutes. Remove from the oven. Coarsely tear the parsley and sprinkle over the top, season with pepper, and serve right away.

Making this lasagna is not as time-consuming as you might think. The noodles do not need to be cooked in advance, and if you prepare the meat sauce ahead, the dish can be assembled quickly before it is baked. You can cut the noodles to fit the pan if needed.

bacon-wrapped pork loin with apples

For the stuffing

2 tablespoons
unsalted butter

2 tablespoons olive oil

½ sweet onion such
as Vidalia, finely diced

1 clove garlic,
finely chopped

1 Granny Smith apple,
cored and diced

½ cup (3 oz/90 g)
golden raisins

Sea salt and cracked
pepper

2 tablespoons finely
chopped fresh sage

2 tablespoons fresh
thyme leaves

½ cup (2 oz/60 g)
dried bread crumbs

1 pork loin roast, about
3 lb (1.5 kg), butterflied

Sea salt and cracked
pepper

6 slices applewood-
smoked bacon

1 cup (8 fl oz/250 ml)
dry white wine

MAKES 6–8 SERVINGS

Preheat the oven to 425°F (220°C).

To make the stuffing, in a 10-inch (25-cm) frying pan over medium heat, melt the butter with the olive oil. Add the onion, garlic, apple, and golden raisins. Season lightly with salt and pepper and add the sage and thyme. Cook, stirring occasionally, until the apple is soft and the mixture is golden brown, about 5 minutes. Stir in the bread crumbs, remove from the heat, and let the stuffing cool slightly.

Lay the pork flat on a work surface and season on both sides with salt and pepper. Spread the stuffing over the pork. Roll up the pork to enclose the stuffing and tie it securely at 4 regular intervals with kitchen string.

Turn the meat seam-side down and wrap the bacon slices, slightly overlapping, along the length of the pork, tucking the ends under to secure. Place the pork in a 9-by-13-inch (23-by-33-cm) pan and pour the wine into the pan around the pork.

Roast for 15 minutes. Reduce the oven temperature to 350°F (180°C) and continue to roast until an instant-read thermometer inserted into the center of the roast reads 140°F (60°C), about 40 minutes. Remove from the oven, cover loosely with foil, and let rest for 15 minutes. Cut into slices and serve right away.

Apples and pork are a classic pairing. The bacon helps keep the roast moist and lends a smoky nuance. This is a dish worthy of company, but it isn't too fussy. To save time, ask your butcher to butterfly the pork.

rhubarb & apple crumble

Butter for greasing

1 lb (500 g) fresh rhubarb, cut into ½-inch (12-mm) pieces, or frozen rhubarb pieces

4 Granny Smith apples, peeled, cored, and cut into ½-inch (12-mm) pieces

¾ cup (6 oz/185 g) granulated sugar

2 tablespoons chopped crystallized ginger

1 tablespoon cornstarch

or

For the topping

1 cup (5 oz/155 g) all-purpose flour

¾ cup (6 oz/185 g) firmly packed dark brown sugar

Pinch salt

½ cup (4 oz/125 g) cold unsalted butter, cut into cubes

½ cup (1½ oz/45 g) rolled oats

MAKES 6–8 SERVINGS

Preheat the oven to 375°F (190°C). Butter a 2-qt (2-l) gratin dish.

Combine the rhubarb, apples, granulated sugar, ginger, and cornstarch in the prepared dish and toss together.

To make the topping, in a bowl, combine the flour, brown sugar, and salt. Add the butter and, using your fingertips, rub the ingredients together until they form small clumps. Stir in the oats. Sprinkle the oat mixture evenly over the fruit.

Bake until the fruit is bubbling and the topping is golden brown and crisp, 45–50 minutes. Remove from the oven and serve right away.

At once both sweet and tart, apples and rhubarb are a delightful combination. Chopped crystallized ginger gives a spicy kick to the crunchy, buttery topping that cloaks the fruit. Serve the crumble hot out of the oven, drizzled with heavy cream, if you like.

cherry clafouti

Butter for greasing

1 lb (500 g) pitted
Bing cherries

½ cup (2½ oz/75 g)
all-purpose flour

⅓ cup (3 oz/90 g)
granulated sugar

Pinch salt

4 large eggs

2 cups (16 fl oz/500 ml)
whole milk

2 teaspoons vanilla
extract

1 cup (5½ oz/170 g)
whole almonds, toasted
and coarsely ground

Confectioners' sugar
for dusting

Whipped cream
for serving

MAKES 6 SERVINGS

Preheat the oven to 375°F (190°C). Butter a 2-qt (2-l) gratin dish.

Arrange the cherries in an even layer in the prepared dish. Set aside.

In a bowl, sift together the flour, granulated sugar, and salt. In another bowl, whisk together the eggs, milk, and vanilla. Make a well in the middle of the dry ingredients, pour in the milk mixture, and whisk until a smooth batter forms. Mix in the ground almonds. Pour evenly over the cherries.

Bake until the top is dark golden brown and the custard has set, about 40 minutes. Remove from the oven and sprinkle with confectioners' sugar. Serve right away, accompanied by whipped cream.

When sweet, juicy cherries are in season, they are just right for this French-style dessert. There are many varieties, but dark ruby Bing cherries are particularly beautiful against the egg custard. For an authentically French clafouti, use unpitted cherries here.

index

weldon**owen**

415 Jackson Street, Suite 200, San Francisco, CA 94111
Telephone: 415 291 0100 Fax: 415 291 8841
www.weldonowen.com

Weldon Owen is a division of

BONNIER

WELDON OWEN, INC.

CEO and President Terry Newell
VP, Sales and Marketing Amy Kaneko
Director of Finance Mark Perrigo

VP and Publisher Hannah Rahill
Executive Editor Jennifer Newens
Editor Donita Boles
Editorial Assistant Becky Duffett

Associate Creative Director Emma Boys
Designer and Illustrator Lauren Charles
Junior Designer Anna Grace

Production Director Chris Hemesath
Production Manager Michelle Duggan
Color Manager Teri Bell

Photographer Ray Kachatorian
Food Stylist Valerie Aikman-Smith
Prop Stylist Christine Wolheim

COOKING IN CAST IRON

Conceived and produced by Weldon Owen, Inc.
Copyright © 2010 Weldon Owen, Inc.

Color separations by Embassy Graphics in Canada
Printed and bound by 1010 Printing, Ltd. in China

First printed in 2010
10 9 8 7 6 5

Library of Congress Cataloging-in-Publication
data is available.

ISBN-13: 978-1-61628-033-8
ISBN-10: 1-61628-033-6

ACKNOWLEDGMENTS

Weldon Owen wishes to thank the following people for their generous support in producing this book:
Kim Chun, Judith Dunham, Alexa Hyman, Ashley Lima, Elizabeth Parson, Lauren Stocker